APR 01 2002   DO:

S0-DYE-201

CELEBRITY BIOS

Ricky Martin

Judy Parker

HIGH
interest
books

Children's Press
A Division of Scholastic Inc.
New York / Toronto / London / Auckland / Sydney
Mexico City / New Delhi / Hong Kong
Danbury, Connecticut

To Ricky's biggest fan in Queens, New York, Luz Celenia Sanchez, with lots of love!

Book Design: Michael DeLisio
Contributing Editors: Eric Fein and Matthew Pitt

Photo Credits: Cover © Retna Ltd.; pp. 4, 7, 10, 16, 38 © Globe Photos Inc.;
pp. 9, 14, 16, 27, 28, 35 © The Everett Collection, Inc.; p. 21 © Corbis;
pp. 23-24, 32 © AP/Wide World Photos; p. 30 © Mitchell Gerber/Corbis;
p. 36 © Joseph Sohm; ChromoSohm Inc./Corbis

Library of Congress Cataloging-in-Publication Data

Parker, Judy.
  Ricky Martin / Judy Parker.
    p. cm. -- (Celebrity bios)
  Includes index.
  ISBN 0-516-23427-7 (lib. bdg.) -- ISBN 0-516-29602-7 (pbk.)
  1. Martin, Ricky--Juvenile literature. 2. Singers--Puerto Rico--Biography--
  Juvenile literature. [1. Martin, Ricky. 2. Singers. 3. Puerto Ricans--
  Biography.] I. Title. II. Series.

ML3930.M328 P37 2001
782.42164'092--dc21
[B]
                                                      00-066045

CONTENTS

CHAPTER ONE

A Young Star

"Menudo was the best school," he told People *magazine in 1995, "all the rehearsals and discipline."*

The date: February 24, 1999. The place: The 41st Annual Grammy Awards show in Los Angeles, California. One performer brings Madonna, Lauryn Hill, Sting, and many others to their feet in a standing ovation. They love his moves, his voice, and his charm. Host Rosie O'Donnell grins and says, "I never heard of him before tonight, but I'm enjoying him so much!" That performer is Ricky Martin!

Ricky Martin was a hit with American music

Even as a youngster, Ricky (bottom left) loved to perform.

fans when he performed at the 1999 Grammy Awards. Many Americans had not heard of Ricky Martin before the televised show. Yet it was love at first sight. The fans loved Ricky's singing and dancing. They were also attracted to his good looks and fun-loving personality. Ricky loved the fans' enthusiasm.

Many people in the United States thought that Ricky was an overnight sensation. But that was not the case. Ricky had sold millions of albums in many other countries. He had fans in Latin America, Asia, and Europe. His performance at the Grammy Awards proved what those fans already knew: Ricky Martin was a superstar.

KIKI

Ricky Martin was born Enrique Martin Morales IV on December 24, 1971, in San Juan, Puerto Rico. As a child he was called Kiki, which means "Little Enrique." His father,

Ricky puts on a colorful costume before he takes the stage.

Enrique Morales III, is a psychologist. His mother is Nereida Morales, an accountant. His mother was married once before she married Ricky's father. So Ricky has two older half brothers, Fernando and Angel. Ricky's parents divorced when he was two years old. After the divorce, Ricky lived with his mother. Ricky's family later included two younger half brothers, Eric and Daniel, and a half sister, Vanessa, from his father's second marriage.

RICKY MARTIN

Puerto Rico is an island and an interesting place to grow up in. To the north of it is the Atlantic Ocean. South of the island is the Caribbean Sea. Most of the people who live in Puerto Rico are Hispanic. Two languages are spoken in Puerto Rico—Spanish and English. There also are many other cultures on the island. Puerto Rican art, dance, and music have been influenced by the cultures of South America, Europe, and the United States.

Ricky always was interested in show business. He liked singing and listening to American bands. Some of his favorite musical groups were Journey, Cheap Trick, and Boston. But his mother didn't want him to forget his Latin roots. She took him to concerts by Latin performers such as singer Celia Cruz and percussionist Tito Puente.

From the time he was a little boy, Ricky dreamed of being a performer. When he was six, he began acting in television commercials. His

By the age of twelve, Ricky (bottom right) was already a full-fledged star in Puerto Rico.

first love, though, was singing. He decided that he wanted to join the musical group Menudo.

TOO SMALL FOR MENUDO

Menudo was an all-boy band from Puerto Rico. They got their start in 1977. The group always was made up of five young men. When a member turned eighteen years old, he was considered too old for the band and had to leave. Auditions were held to replace outgoing members of the band.

Menudo gave young Ricky (top left) his first sweet taste of success.

Ricky first auditioned for Menudo in 1984 when he was twelve years old. He was rejected because he was too short, yet Ricky didn't give up. He started playing basketball, hoping that it would make him taller. It didn't work. He auditioned again, and again he was rejected.

A Young Star

Finally, on his third try, Ricky impressed the group's producers with his determination. "He was small, and his voice was not so good then," the manager of Menudo told *Time International* magazine, "but we thought he could learn a lot by being with [Menudo]." At age twelve, Ricky flew from San Juan, Puerto Rico, to Miami, Florida, to begin training for Menudo.

Menudo was a challenging experience for Ricky. His days were filled with long hours of rehearsals. The group practiced singing and dancing so they would be perfect when they performed. Ricky's hard work paid off. Menudo's managers recognized Ricky's talent, and made him lead singer.

Soon, Ricky was touring the world. Menudo performed in many different countries, including Japan, Brazil, and the Philippines. Over the next five years, Ricky became a professional performer. His popularity grew and grew.

DIFFICULT DECISIONS

The Menudo years were hard on Ricky and his family. He toured a lot, so he didn't get home very often. His parents began to fight over who would spend time with him at home. Ricky felt that he was being forced to choose between his father and his mother. The pressure from his father became too much. Ricky stopped talking to him in 1985. He didn't speak to his father for almost ten years. Meanwhile, Ricky continued to tour with Menudo. Before long, his mother wasn't happy that he was away from home so much. "My career," Ricky told *People*, "destroyed my family."

Ricky's experiences during his Menudo years were wild and crazy. It was easy for the popular band to meet girls. Their manager, Edgardo Diaz, became very strict to keep the band under control. This was hard for fun-loving Ricky and the rest of the band. They also felt that their creativity was being stifled. They started to question the need for rehearsing the same routines over and over.

Ricky left Menudo in 1989 when he was seventeen years old. He spent the next eight months at home in San Juan, Puerto Rico. During that time, he graduated from high school. Ricky thought he might stay in Puerto Rico and go to college. He considered becoming

Did you know?

Ricky Martin is left-handed!

a pediatrician (a children's doctor). Instead, he moved to Queens, New York, in 1990.

In New York City, Ricky was able to stay with friends. He lived on the money he had saved from working with Menudo. One year later, Ricky moved to Mexico.

Ricky gives his all with each and every song.

A RISING STAR

In 1991, Ricky arrived in Mexico. He worked on a television soap opera. The show was called "Alcanzar una Estrella" ("Reach for a Star"). Though he became a popular TV star, he missed singing. His success with Menudo helped Ricky get a recording contract with Sony Records. He recorded his first solo album in Spanish.

A Young Star

The first album was titled *Ricky Martin*. Ricky co-wrote the songs with his friend Robi Rosa. Like Ricky, Robi had been a member of Menudo. Ricky Martin was a success on the Latin music charts. Ricky's fans from his Menudo days still loved him. As his singing career took off again, Ricky continued acting. He had a part in the movie version of "Alcanzar una Estrella."

In 1993, Ricky recorded his second Spanish-language album, *Me Amaras (You Will Love Me)*. The album was a big hit. Together, Ricky's first two albums sold 1.5 million copies worldwide.

BACK TO AMERICA

Ricky's success in Latin America brought him some attention in the United States. In 1994, the producers of the soap opera "General Hospital" hired Ricky. They cast him in the role of a bartender named Miguel Morez. Ricky had a lot in common with his character. Miguel was a Puerto

Working on "General Hospital" gave Ricky (second from left) the chance to both sing and act.

Rican singer. This gave Ricky the chance to sing on the television series. "General Hospital" fans loved Ricky and sent him tons of mail.

After a year of playing Miguel Morez, Ricky was ready to move on. He tried out for the role of Marius in the hit Broadway musical *Les Miserables*. The character Marius is an idealistic student rebelling against the French government. Ricky got the part. He spent most of 1996 living in New York City and playing Marius. "I gave my best [as Marius]," Ricky told the Spanish magazine *Eres*, "and in exchange

I received a lot of credibility as an artist."

Ricky continued to build on his popularity by releasing his third Spanish-language album, *A Medio Vivir (Not Living a Full Life)*. The album came out in September 1995. By October, it went gold, selling half a million copies.

A Medio Vivir was a step in a new musical direction. Ricky's first two albums had mostly pop songs. With *A Medio Vivir*, he began to experiment with a harder rock sound. The single "Maria," from the album, became the number one song in twenty-eight countries.

Ricky had thrilled fans in many countries with his music. Now he wanted to break into the Top 40 charts in the United States. His appearances on American television and Broadway had earned him some recognition. He was ready to move to the next level. Ricky Martin was about to become a household name in the United States.

CHAPTER TWO

Conquering the World

*"The percussion makes everybody dance,"
Ricky told MTV. "Even though I'm changing
languages, I'm not changing the sounds. I'm
presenting myself as who I am."*

ALMOST A SUPERSTAR

In 1997, Ricky was twenty-five years old. For
most of his life, he had performed and toured,
making music that he loved. Ricky was recognized in most of the world as a great performer.
Yet he still dreamed of having a hit in the United
States. Ricky planned his career carefully. His

By the time Ricky turned twenty-five, he already was a success.

first two albums established him in Latin America. His third album also made him popular in Europe and Asia. "America is like my doctorate degree," Ricky told *Rolling Stone.* "Europe and Asia [are where] I did my master's."

Soon, Ricky got more exposure. The Walt Disney Company asked him to work on the animated movie *Hercules.* Ricky recorded the voice of Hercules for the Spanish-language soundtrack of the movie. He also sang the theme from *Hercules,* "No Importa La Distancia" ("Go the Distance").

After working with Disney, Ricky recorded his fourth album, *Vuelve (Return).* On *Vuelve,* Ricky combined his love of Latin music with his love of American rock and pop. *Vuelve* featured dance tunes with Latin percussion and horns. It also included beautiful pop ballads.

Before releasing the album, Ricky released a single, "La Bomba" ("The Bomb"). It became

Ricky is all smiles as he signs copies of his fourth album, *Vuelve*.

an instant international hit. By the time *Vuelve* came out in February 1998, his fans were eager to buy the album. *Vuelve* went gold in July. It got great reviews from American critics. *Billboard* magazine said the album was full of potential hits. *Vibe* magazine said, "*Vuelve* reflects Ricky Martin's evolution into a well-seasoned artist."

RICKY MARTIN

Ricky began a world tour to support the album. During the first half of 1998, the *Vuelve* tour went to Japan, Argentina, Spain, France, Greece, Israel, Turkey, and many other countries. Ricky performed "La Copa de la Vida" ("The Cup of Life") at the World Cup soccer match. The audience for the World Cup was two billion people! The song went on to become the number one single in more than thirty countries.

Ricky's world tour continued in the fall of 1998 with concerts in the United States. In December, the tour moved to Asia. Ricky became the first Hispanic artist to perform in Beijing, China. In Singapore, Ricky was the first person to perform under a new law that allowed audiences to stand up and dance. The *Vuelve* tour was a huge success. Ricky felt that the time was now right for an English-language album. He recorded the album that would be released the following summer.

Ricky loves to please his adoring fans.

Ricky shows off his Grammy Award.

PERFORMANCE OF A LIFETIME

Ricky got his big American break when he performed "La Copa de la Vida" ("The Cup of Life") at the 1999 Grammy Awards show. It was a classic Ricky Martin performance. He drove the audience crazy and received a standing ovation at the end of his number.

There was even more success for Ricky that night. *Vuelve* won the Grammy Award for Best Latin Pop Performance. At the press conference, Ricky met reporters. He proudly showed off his Grammy Award. Suddenly, someone came up behind him. She covered his eyes to surprise him. It was Madonna. She wanted to congratulate him. That night, they decided to record a song together for his next record.

LIVING *LA VIDA LOCA*

After Ricky's performance at the Grammys, the sales of *Vuelve* shot up by 400 percent. The album hit *Billboard*'s Hot 100. In April, the album went platinum, selling one million copies.

Ricky's record company, Sony Music, knew they needed to bring out his English-language album soon. They decided to release the album in May 1999 instead of later that year.

RICKY MARTIN

Ricky named his first English-language album *Ricky Martin*, even though his first Spanish-language album had had the same title. He worked with talented producers such as Jon Secada and Desmond Child. Ricky and Madonna worked quickly to record their duet, "Be Careful." William Orbit, the producer of Madonna's Grammy-winning album *Ray of Light*, produced the duet. The song was produced in Madonna's California studio. Ricky flew back and forth between his home in Miami and the studio in Los Angeles. He was very happy with the results. "It came out amazing!" Ricky told *Miami Metro*. "The song is a journey. It's gorgeous!"

In April, the first single from the album *Ricky Martin* was released. The song "Livin' La Vida Loca" ("Living the Crazy Life") hit the number one spot on *Billboard*'s Hot 100. It sold more copies than any other single in 1999.

After singing "Livin' La Vida Loca," Ricky listens to
the wild applause.

Ricky has a serious side, too.

The song created great word-of-mouth for Ricky's upcoming album. "Livin' La Vida Loca" was a very important song for Ricky. The song climbed the charts everywhere, including MTV's "Total Request Live." The song reflected the wild energy of Ricky's new success. It allowed him to connect with the fans who loved his music most. "I want them to feel free," Ricky told VH1. "I want them to be who they are with my music."

Conquering the World

On May 11, 1999, the album *Ricky Martin* was released. It immediately became the number one album in the United States. It also was number one in Canada, Australia, Japan, Spain, and in many other countries. When Sony Music announced the dates for Ricky's U.S. tour, tickets sold out within an hour.

Awards started pouring in for both *Vuelve* and *Ricky Martin*. *Vuelve* won two *Billboard* Latin Music Awards. The video for "Livin' La Vida Loca" won Best Dance Video and Best Pop Video at the 1999 MTV Video Music Awards. Ricky also won honors at the World Music Awards, the Teen Choice Awards, and the American Latino Media Arts Awards. Ricky even won the MTV Russian Viewers' Choice Award.

Ricky's dreams were coming true. He had conquered the United States and the rest of the world. Everywhere he went, Ricky thrilled fans

with his electrifying performances. In an interview with *Time* magazine, Ricky summed up how he felt. "What, are you kidding me?" he said. "I'm flying! I'm flying!"

Did you know?

Ricky Martin was one of *People*'s 50 Most Beautiful People two years in a row (1999 and 2000).

Ricky has his hands full with awards from MTV.

CHAPTER THREE

A Man of Style

"For me, it's very important to be centered and focused," Ricky told Teen People. *"That is the only way that you will survive."*

FASHION FLAIR

Ricky always has been a great-looking guy. As his popularity has grown, many people have noticed his unique style. In 1999, Ricky was on *People*'s 10 Best-Dressed List. He also was featured in a sexy photo layout in *W*, a fashion magazine.

Most of Ricky's clothes are designed by Giorgio Armani. The Armani look is hip but classic.

Ricky is one of the world's best-dressed singers.

COPING WITH FAME

Ricky loves his crazy life. Yet he has learned to take good care of himself. Desmond Child, one of the producers of *Ricky Martin*, told *Teen People*, "All [Ricky] needs is a good night's sleep, and he's ready to go."

Did you know?

Ricky was nominated for the Most Fashionable Artist Award at the VH1 Fashion Awards.

Of course, it takes more than just a good night's sleep to stay healthy. Ricky makes sure that he takes time for himself every day. He uses the time to think about his life and focus on his goals. Ricky always eats breakfast alone. Some of his favorite breakfast foods are pancakes, yogurt, and raisin-bran cereal.

Another way Ricky stays focused is through yoga. Yoga is a gentle exercise for the mind and body. Yoga was developed hundreds of years ago in the Hindu and Buddhist religions. Ricky is able to use yoga to relax and focus.

In addition, yoga has helped Ricky stay in touch with his spirituality. Spirituality is very important to Ricky. "[In yoga] you're sitting comfortably, stretching your back . . . you're listening to your body, to your natural sounds," Ricky explained to *Miami Metro*.

Ricky relaxes before a big show.

NO TIME FOR LOVE

Ricky's busy schedule has left him no time for romance. "I am romantic," Ricky told MTV

With its hot weather and warm residents, Miami is the perfect hometown for Ricky.

Europe. In 1989, Ricky met Rebecca de Alba, a television journalist. They were together, off and on, for the next ten years. Unfortunately, they broke up in 1999. Ricky was sad, but he knew he would fall in love again one day. "My lack of a girlfriend is not because I travel a lot," he told *TV Hits* magazine. "It's more about not having met the right person."

Ricky isn't lonely, though. He has very close friends with whom he keeps in touch. Many of those friends are people he has known for more than fifteen years. Some of them travel with

Ricky when he is on tour. Ricky also is very close to his family. In 1996, after almost ten years of being angry at each other, Ricky and his father made up. Today, Ricky and his father are friends.

FOOD AND ART

Music is the center of Ricky's life. Yet he also has other interests. In 1998, Ricky opened a Puerto Rican restaurant in the South Beach section of Miami. The restaurant is called Casa Salsa. It has been very successful. During his U.S.A. tour press conference, Ricky talked about Casa Salsa. He said, "You feel like you have walked into a modern Puerto Rican house, offering you live music and tropical rhythms." Ricky created Casa Salsa with the people who own Ajili Mojili, his favorite restaurant in Puerto Rico. "It reminds me so much of the food my grandmother used to cook for me," Ricky said of Ajili Mojili at the press conference.

Between projects Ricky takes time out to relax.

Ricky is also an art collector. He likes many different artists, including the Chinese-Cuban painter Wilfredo Lam, the Colombian sculptor and painter Fernando Botero, and the Nicaraguan printmaker Armando Morales. He has works by these artists in his home in Miami.

MORE IN STORE

Ricky went back into the studio in early 2000. It was time to record his second English-language album, *Sound Loaded*. The first single,

A Man of Style

"She Bangs," was another energetic pop tune. It was a perfect dance song. Again, Ricky worked with talented producers. Gloria Estefan's husband, Emilio, produced several tracks on *Sound Loaded*. Ricky also worked with one of Mariah Carey's producers, Walter Afanasieff.

Sound Loaded was released in November 2000. It was the number four album on the *Billboard* chart in its first week. The album got great reviews, too. *Rolling Stone* magazine said that *Sound Loaded* was very "likable and danceable." *Billboard* magazine said that Ricky's album featured "well-crafted material on which he's allowed to truly strut his vocal stuff."

Thanks to *Sound Loaded*, Ricky again is able to share Latin music. He is an incredible performer who excites and inspires fans all over the world. Because of Ricky, people everywhere love Latin music. As all his fans know, Ricky will continue to be a big star.

TIMELINE

1971
- Ricky Martin is born on December 24.

1984
- Ricky joins Menudo after two previous auditions.

1991
- Ricky's first album, *Ricky Martin,* is released.

1993
- Ricky's album *Me Amaras* is released.

1994
- Ricky joins the cast of "General Hospital" as Miguel Morez. Ricky stars in the Broadway show *Les Miserables.*

1995
- Ricky's album *A Medio Vivir* is released in September. By October, *A Medio Vivir* goes gold.

1998
- Ricky's album *Vuelve* is released, featuring the single "La Copa de la Vida." In July, *Vuelve* goes gold.

TIMELINE

1999   • Ricky wins the Grammy Award for Best Latin Pop Performance for *Vuelve*.
At the Grammy Award ceremony in February, Ricky stuns the crowd with his live performance of "The Cup of Life."
In May, Ricky releases his first English-language album, *Ricky Martin*, which includes a duet with Madonna.

2000   • In November, Ricky releases his second English-language album, *Sound Loaded*.

FACT SHEET

Name	Enrique Martin Morales IV
Nicknames	Ricky, Kiki
Born	December 24, 1971
Birthplace	San Juan, Puerto Rico
Family	Mother, Nereida Morales; Father, Enrique Martin Morales III
Sign	Capricorn
Height	6'1"
Hair	Dark brown
Eyes	Brown

Favorites

Pets	Titan, a Chihuahua; Icaro, a golden retriever
Tattoos	On his hip, a rose with a bleeding purple heart
Songs	Sting's "Fragile," Miguel Bose's "Dende"
Singers	Miguel Bose
Foods	Cuban, Italian, Mexican
Movies	*The Godfather*
Actor	Robert De Niro

NEW WORDS

audition to try out for something

Billboard's Hot 100 the top-selling recordings listed by *Billboard* magazine

Broadway the part of New York City in which live theaters are located

chart a listing that ranks music sales

duet a song for two performers

gold record certificate awarded to a record that sells half a million (500,000) copies

Grammy an award given in recognition of musical achievement

pediatrician a doctor who treats children

percussion instruments such as drums

platinum record certificate awarded to a record that sells one million copies

producer the person who supervises the production of a record, film, or television program

rehearsal practice for a performance

soundtrack the music recorded for a movie

studio a place where music is recorded

NEW WORDS

Top 40 the forty most popular or best-selling
   recordings

World Cup the championship soccer game
   played by teams from many different countries

FOR FURTHER READING

Duncan, Patricia J. *Ricky Martin: La Vida Loca*. New York: Warner Books, Incorporated, 1999.

Krulik, Nancy E. *Ricky Martin: Rockin' the House*. New York: Simon & Schuster Trade, 1999.

Marerro, Letisha. *Ricky Martin: Unauthorized Biography*. San Francisco, CA: Harper San Francisco, 1999.

Sparks, Kristin. *Ricky Martin: Livin' La Vida Loca*. New York: The Berkley Publishing Group, 1999.

RESOURCES

Web Sites

www.rmlac.com
Home to the U.S. Ricky Martin fan club, it includes interviews, articles, and much more!

www.rickymartin.com
This is the Official Ricky Martin Web site from his record company.

www.rockonthenet.com
This site offers great information about Ricky and many other artists.

Fan Club
Ricky Martin International Fan Club
P.O. BOX 13345, Santurce Station
San Juan, Puerto Rico 00908-3345

INDEX

About the Author

Judy Parker has written on a variety of subjects for young adults. She is a Latin music fan and loves to dance salsa.